VIOLENT VOLCANOES

by Noah Leatherland

Minneapolis, Minnesota

Credits
Images are courtesy of Shutterstock.com. With thanks to Getty Images, Thinkstock Photo, and iStockphoto. Cover – DanielFreyr, oldravvv. Recurring – hugolacasse, donatas1205. 2–3 – Fast_Cyclone. 4–5 – ESB Professional, BMJ. 6–7 – LukaKikina, Saintdags. 8–9 – ONYXprj, Nikolay Zaborskikh. 10–11 – Athanasios Doumas, Nsit. 12–13 – Lucy.Brown, Islamic Footage. 14–15 – Aleksandar Todorovic, stephen reich. 16–17 – Evgeny Haritonov, Fishman64. 18–19 – JackKPhoto, Oleg Elkov. 20–21 – Skylines, speedshutter Photography. 22–23 – Florian Nimsdorf, Jakub Maculewicz.

Bearport Publishing Company Product Development Team
Publisher: Jen Jenson; Director of Product Development: Spencer Brinker; Editorial Director: Allison Juda; Editor: Cole Nelson; Editor: Tiana Tran; Production Editor: Naomi Reich; Art Director: Kim Jones; Designer: Kayla Eggert; Designer: Steve Scheluchin; Production Specialist: Owen Hamlin

Library of Congress Cataloging-in-Publication Data is available at www.loc.gov or upon request from the publisher.

ISBN: 979-8-89577-081-8 (hardcover)
ISBN: 979-8-89577-528-8 (paperback)
ISBN: 979-8-89577-198-3 (ebook)

© 2026 BookLife Publishing
This edition is published by arrangement with BookLife Publishing.

North American adaptations © 2026 Bearport Publishing Company. All rights reserved. No part of this publication may be reproduced in whole or in part, stored in any retrieval system, or transmitted in any form or by any means, electronic, mechanical, photocopying, recording, or otherwise, without written permission from the publisher. Bearport Publishing is a division of FlutterBee Education Group.

For more information, write to Bearport Publishing, 3500 American Blvd W, Suite 150, Bloomington, MN 55431.

CONTENTS

Our Home 4

Volcanoes 6

Making a Volcano 8

Volcano Parts. 10

Eruptions .12

Dealing Damage. 14

Volcanologists 16

Daring Data 18

Staying Safe 20

Safe Studies 22

Glossary 24

Index 24

OUR HOME

Check out our home planet, Earth! It has everything we need to live. However, not everything on Earth is very nice. . . .

Earth can sometimes be a dangerous place. Some things on our planet can **damage** land and buildings. Others can cause death!

River rapids

LET'S LEARN ABOUT VIOLENT VOLCANOES!

VOLCANOES

Volcanoes are openings at Earth's **surface**. They are places where hot rock and **gases** can escape. Volcanoes often look like mountains or hills.

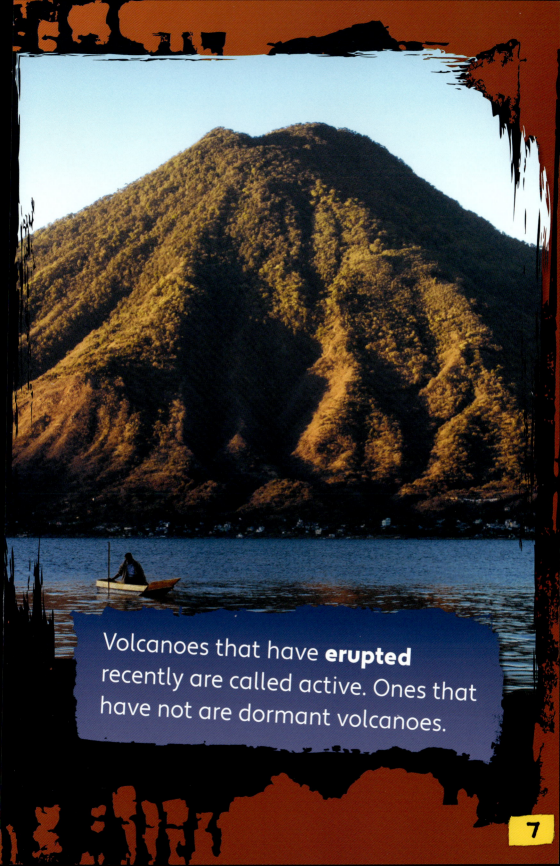

Volcanoes that have **erupted** recently are called active. Ones that have not are dormant volcanoes.

MAKING A VOLCANO

How do volcanoes form? Earth has different layers. The rocky crust is the outer layer. Underneath it is the mantle.

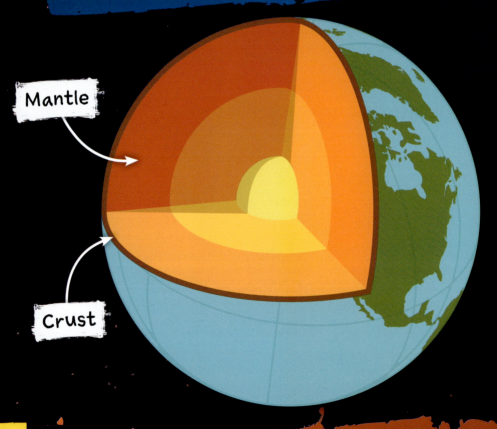

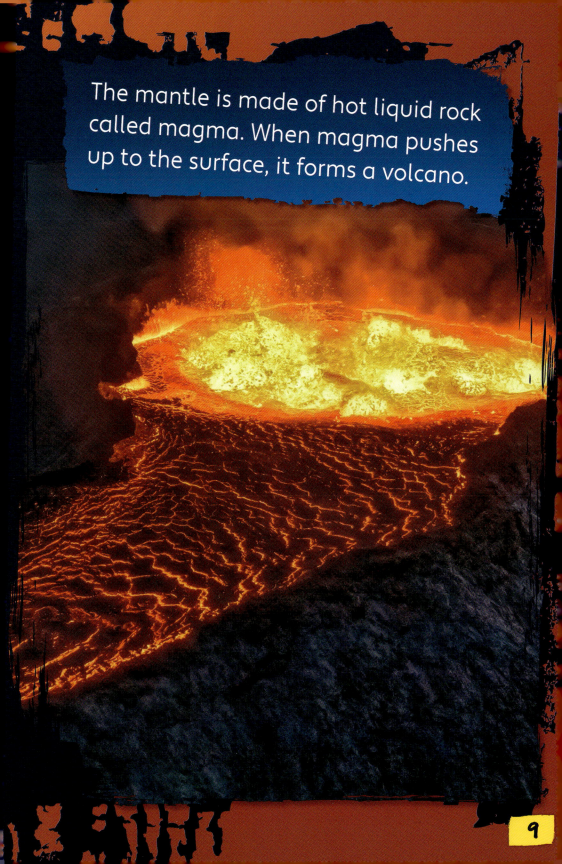

The mantle is made of hot liquid rock called magma. When magma pushes up to the surface, it forms a volcano.

VOLCANO PARTS

Volcanoes have many different parts. The opening of a volcano is the vent. Around the vent is an area called the crater.

Crater

Vent

Magma is held underground in the chamber. The tube to the vent is called the conduit.

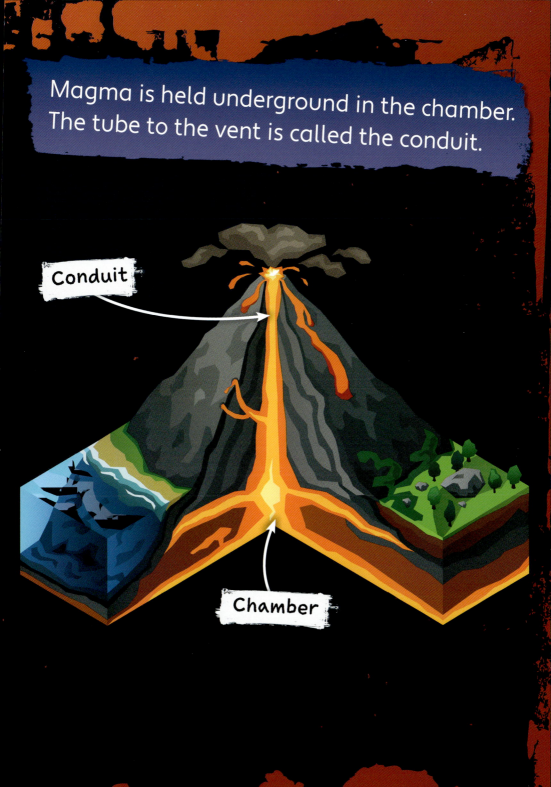

ERUPTIONS

When a volcano explodes, it is called an eruption (i-RUP-shun). *Boom!* The volcano shoots out ash, gas, and rock.

When magma reaches Earth's surface, it is called lava. It can be runny or thick.

Lava

DEALING DAMAGE

Volcanic eruptions cause lots of damage. Lava can burn almost anything it touches!

Gas and ash in the air after eruptions are dangerous. They can make it hard to breathe and may even cause death.

VOLCANOLOGISTS

Volcanologists (vol-KAY-noh-luh-jists) are scientists who study volcanoes. They find out how and why volcanoes erupt.

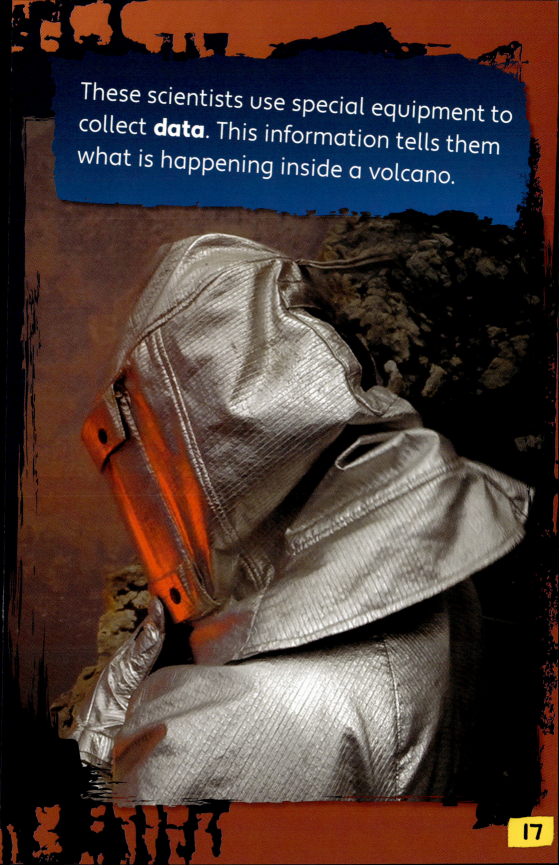

These scientists use special equipment to collect **data**. This information tells them what is happening inside a volcano.

DARING DATA

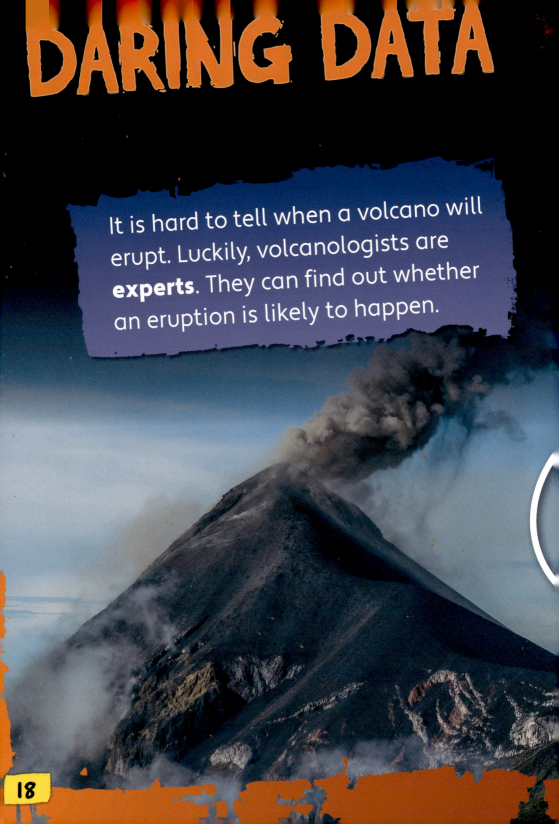

It is hard to tell when a volcano will erupt. Luckily, volcanologists are **experts**. They can find out whether an eruption is likely to happen.

If a volcano might erupt, volcanologists send out warnings. These messages help people prepare to keep safe.

STAYING SAFE

What should you do during a volcano warning? Listen to instructions to keep safe. Pack canned food and water.

Keep a radio nearby. If an eruption happens, the warning will tell you what to do. Some people might have to leave their homes to go somewhere safer.

SAFE STUDIES

Volcanoes are super interesting to learn about. However, they can be very dangerous.

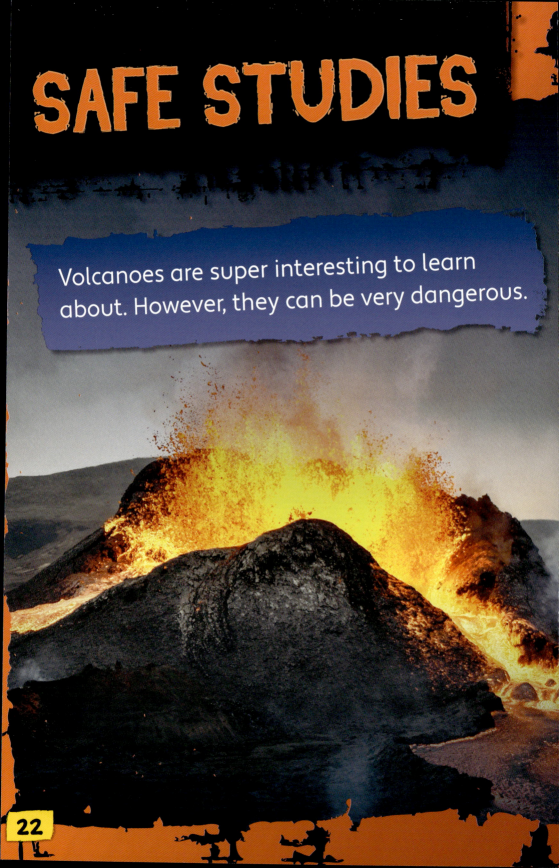

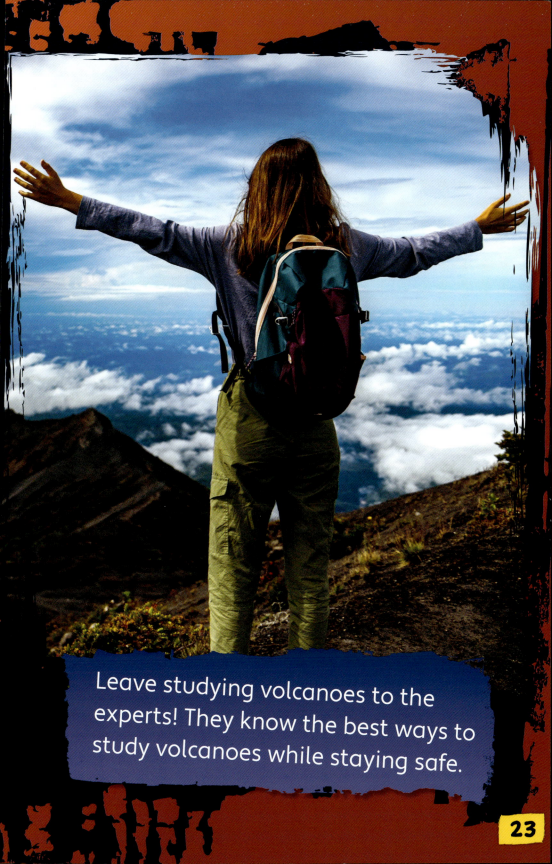

Leave studying volcanoes to the experts! They know the best ways to study volcanoes while staying safe.

GLOSSARY

damage harm

data information based on facts and numbers

erupted sent out very hot melted rock and gases in a sudden explosion

experts people who know a lot about a subject

gases things that spread out to fill any space available

surface the top layer of something

INDEX

ash 12, 15
data 17–18
eruptions 7, 12, 14–16, 18–19, 21
gases 6, 12, 15
lava 12–14
layers 8
magma 9, 11, 13
radio 21
rocks 6, 8–9, 12
volcanologists 16, 18–19